JESUS IN THE GOSPELS

JESUS IN THE GOSPELS

Handbook

DISCIPLE
Second Generation Studies

יֵשׁוּ

Name Him Jesus. The name *Jesus* appears on the cover in both Hebrew and Greek. The large letters are ancient Hebrew script and come from an inscription. They spell the name *Yeshu*, *Jesus*, and are to be read from right to left. *Yesu*, *Yeshu*, *Yeshua*, *Yehoshua* are English forms of the Hebrew/Aramaic name *Joshua*, which means "God is salvation." Matthew 1:18-22, printed in Greek over the representations of four manuscript pages, includes the words that translate into English as "you are to name him Jesus." *Iesous* is the English spelling of the Greek name *Jesus*. The Greek form of the name, as used in Matthew 1:21, appears in darker type. The four manuscript pages suggest the four Gospels. Of the four Gospels only Matthew and Luke include the instruction to "name him Jesus."

Ιησουν

DISCIPLE **Second Generation Studies.** JESUS IN THE GOSPELS is the first study in a line of projected studies different from but also related in some ways to DISCIPLE Bible study. This new line is called DISCIPLE Second Generation Studies. The nature of the relationship to DISCIPLE touches on such things as language used to describe the program, training requirement, availability to DISCIPLE-enrolled churches, expectation of disciplined daily study, approach to learning, and commitment to attendance and participation in weekly group study.

While distinct in format and approach to study, this new generation of Bible study materials builds on the foundation and carries forward the philosophy and the ideals that shaped DISCIPLE—high commitment, long-term, disciplined study.

DISCIPLE Second Generation Studies are text-based with attention given in daily reading assignments to Old Testament and New Testament Scriptures. Format and design of print and video components will differ from but have some family resemblance to DISCIPLE. All Second Generation Studies will carry their own title but will be identified on the covers as belonging to DISCIPLE Second Generation Studies. Completion of DISCIPLE: BECOMING DISCIPLES THROUGH BIBLE STUDY is prerequisite for JESUS IN THE GOSPELS and for future Second Generation Studies.

JESUS IN THE GOSPELS is different from DISCIPLE Bible study in its approach to Scripture—it looks more closely at the Gospel texts, in the kind of daily preparation and study required of participants, in lesson layout and design, and in the nature of the study and discussion that takes place in the weekly group meeting.

JESUS IN THE GOSPELS focuses on the portraits of Jesus found in the four Gospels—Matthew, Mark, Luke, and John. The word *in* used in the title signals that this study takes an approach different from the familiar "life and teaching of Jesus" approach of reading stories and accounts of what Jesus said and did in order to draw conclusions about their meaning and about who Jesus was. *This study looks at the way each Gospel writer presents events and teachings and at the picture of Jesus that emerges in each of the Gospels.*

The Gospel of Mark provides the framework for the study and in most lessons provides the lead passage to which are added accounts of the same story or event from the other Gospels and supportive Scriptures from the Old Testament and other parts of the New Testament.

Unlike DISCIPLE, this study is not divided into lessons on the Old Testament and lessons on the New Testament; rather, daily assignments for most lessons include Old Testament and New Testament passages. The passages assigned from the Old Testament are important for the Gospel readings. From time to time, readings from the Apocrypha are included to aid understanding of the Jewish thought-world Jesus inherited.

Lessons 1–22 concentrate on the Synoptic Gospels with some related passages from John. Lessons 23–30 concentrate on the Gospel of John with supporting passages from other parts of the New Testament and the Old Testament. In the course of the thirty weeks, participants will read the four Gospels and considerable amounts of Scripture from other parts of the Bible.

To Know Who Jesus Is, We Must Study the Jesus in the Gospels. The four canonical portraits of Jesus—the heart of this study—focus on Jesus himself by the ways they situate him in time and place.

Attention to *name* and *place* and *people* suggests particularity and historical rootedness:

Name—The narratives retain the personal name *Jesus*. While some references in the Gospels are to *Christ* and *Lord*, the Gospels consistently refer to *Jesus*. The name is not replaced by christological expressions. Actually, the Gospels are christology in story form.

Place—The Galilee of Herod is the Galilee of Jesus, and the Jerusalem of the Temple and of Pilate is the Jerusalem of Jesus. Concern for place in the Resurrection points to concern for historical rootedness.

People—Ancestry places Jesus within a people and points to the basis of his authority. His interactions with specific persons—women, tax collectors, Pharisees, children—convey his impact on daily life.

The history-rooted Jesus in the Gospels challenges preconceived ideas about Jesus. For those who think of Jesus as merely an intriguing figure from the past, the historical and canonical portraits of Jesus will show them the Jesus who is more than a figure to be memorialized.

Participants in JESUS IN THE GOSPELS will encounter the Jesus who is both hard to ignore and hard to control—an attractive, commanding, morally compelling figure. It is that Jesus who is Lord and Savior, friend.

The Gospels Are Proclamation Not Neutral Reporting. They arise out of allegiance to Jesus and they call the reader to allegiance to Jesus. They are not concerned with presenting what is usually thought of as biography. The Gospels' aim is to form their readers by the way they inform them about the subject matter—Jesus. This Jesus is from faith to faith.

The Gospels reveal a multifaceted Jesus, not a monolithic figure; not a single portrait but four portraits of Jesus. Each Gospel writer attempts to capture some aspect or element about Jesus but does not capture everything. And it is not possible to combine the aspects or elements of all four portraits into a single picture. Different handling of the materials by the Gospel writers enhances the portraits. The task of the reader and of this study is to discover the different accents of the Gospel writers.

In all four Gospels the reader is in on the story of Jesus in a way that the characters in the Gospels themselves are not. In other words, the reader is always looking over the shoulder of the Gospel writers. Readers are faced with the question, "Who is Jesus for me?" as were the original hearers.

Because knowledge of the Old Testament is necessary for understanding the Gospels, participants in the study of JESUS IN THE GOSPELS must have completed DISCIPLE: BECOMING DISCIPLES THROUGH BIBLE STUDY.

Each Gospel Has a Distinctive Angle of Vision. Most readers of Scripture tend to read the Gospels and put the stories together into one story—one Jesus. But that one Jesus is not the church's Jesus. The church has never substituted a single story for the Jesus of the four Gospels. Each Gospel's way of presenting Jesus and his significance reflects not just the writer's view of Jesus and events but also reflects what was going on in the writer's church. These differences in perspective on Jesus provide opportunities to understand and appropriate more than one way of following Jesus.

This study lets each Gospel have its say so that each Gospel's witness to Jesus might challenge the reader in its own way. As participants in this study read Scripture and related materials, they will grow increasingly alert to the view of Jesus being presented in each Gospel and in each week's Scripture.

How Something Is Told Reflects Why It Is Told. The first question to ask in studying Bible stories or accounts of events is not, What happened? but What do the stories want to tell us through what they report and how they report it?

Time and again this study asks participants to put aside the questions they usually ask of Scripture because the questions are not "gospel questions"; that is, questions that point to the good news of Jesus as God's gift by which humanity can be restored to God's intent. The right questions for our own discipleship. We look for what the Gospel writers are telling us and for the kind of responses they seem to expect of us.

Again—how something is told reflects why it is told. Sometimes the Gospel writers report what Jesus said and did in almost the same way. At other times they tell the same story differently or put it at a different place in the Gospel or sometimes in a different setting. JESUS IN THE GOSPELS uses these differences in how something is told to detect some aspect of what each Gospel writer wants to highlight about Jesus. That is, each Gospel has its own way of confronting the reader with Jesus himself. So we read each Gospel carefully.

Reading Is Not Passive. Many DISCIPLE graduates who come to this study will have studied the life and teaching of Jesus or the life and ministry of Jesus, but few will ever have studied Jesus in the various ways the Gospels present him. This approach to study of the Gospels requires and involves the participant in close reading of the text—not to be done on the run, in bits and pieces, or at the last minute. The Bible discloses its meanings to those who stay with it long enough to get something out of it.

Reading with the Bible, the study manual, and the Gospel Comparisons open and checking and comparing references as they occur will produce meaning to a degree that simply reading without comparing cannot.

Close reading of the Gospel texts is like studying a portrait up close. Different aspects of the painting come to attention according to the focus of that close look. Each week readers will write their conclusions about what has emerged for them from their close reading of the Gospels. Readers will write their descriptions of the Jesus who confronted them in each lesson.

Reading for detail means being present to the text, making oneself accessible to the text—and risking being changed by the text.

Everything Needed for Challenging Study: study manual, Gospel Comparisons, video component, leader guide, certificate, and cross. We recommend use of a New Revised Standard Version study Bible.

Study Manual. Guides daily study and preparation for the weekly group meeting. The main elements in the format are designated by scriptural phrases:

"They have no wine" (John 2:3) is a brief statement about the human condition and alerts the reader to some aspect of daily life that needs help.

"Beginning with Moses and all the prophets" (Luke 24:27) is a way of referring to Scripture as a whole and signals the fact that to understand Jesus in the Gospels we must attend to the Old Testament.

"Do you want to become his disciples, too?" (John 9:27, New International Version) is designed to stimulate thoughtful reflection so readers can come to their own conclusions about what their own discipleship calls for.

The title of each lesson also functions as the heading for the commentary portion of the lesson in the study manual.

Accompanying each day's Scripture reading assignments are suggestions of things to look for that take the reader deeper into Scripture. The words *note* and *observe* are used often in the suggestions to encourage close attention to detail. These suggestions are placed with each day's assignments where they will best influence reading and study. In *noting* and *observing* carefully, readers may discover things in the text they might otherwise have missed. These suggestions sometimes amount to two or three sentences; other times, several sentences. As the study progresses, suggestions of things to look for increase in length and detail in order to develop the participant's ability to read carefully.

As readers become aware of detail in Scripture, they might ask themselves repeatedly, What am I to make of this? The study manual provides space for writing notes on insights, observations, and questions related to the Scripture, and for putting into words personal perceptions of Jesus from the week's Scripture.

Study manual layout and design contribute to discipline in study and provide guidance in reading Scripture for detail. Occasional use of different ink colors allows emphasis on particular content and enables quick visual comparison of Gospel words, phrases, or verses.

JESUS IN THE GOSPELS *Content*

Study manual content confronts the reader weekly with some aspect of the Jesus in the Gospels and connects Scripture to daily life and Jesus' call to discipleship.

The overarching aim is to deepen discipleship through better understanding of the biblical texts and their message. The study reinforces understanding that Jesus is rooted in Judaism and the Scriptures of Judaism and that Christianity and the New Testament are rooted in the Scriptures of Judaism—our Old Testament.

1. Jesus *in* the Gospels
2. When Words Became Events
3. Celebrating Beginnings
4. The Wilderness Voice
5. Gifted by the Spirit and Tested by Choices
6. When God's Reign Becomes Real
7. Called and Commissioned
8. Mission With Healing Power
9. Conflicts Over Obedience

11

Prayers. The prayers accompanying the lessons in the study manual are taken from Psalms and are quoted from The Contemporary English Version. The freshness of this readable and understandable translation makes it especially useful for prayer.

Notes/Charts/Glossary. Topics that cannot be treated within the body of the lesson but are pertinent to the subject matter of the lesson, such as historical information or explanation of a concept, will appear as brief notes or in chart form with the lesson to which they relate. Not every lesson will have such additional information. The study manual also includes a glossary of unfamiliar terms. An asterisk identifies the first mention in the text of each word found in the glossary.

Gospel Comparisons. Selected Gospel portions from the New Revised Standard Version are printed in a multicolumn format to facilitate comparison of similarities and differences in Gospel accounts. The printed selections follow the sequence of Scripture treated in the study manual. This component is a companion to the study manual and functions both in daily study and in group study. Every participant needs a copy of both the study manual and the Gospel Comparisons.

The Gospel portions chosen for inclusion in study teach readers how the same story or event often is reported differently from Gospel to Gospel. Differences in Gospel accounts enrich reader understanding of both the event and the Jesus who emerges in the report of the event. Gospel Comparisons offers ready access to printed accounts of the same story or event. It reduces flipping back and forth among the Gospels in the Bible while comparing passages during daily individual study and weekly group study.

Instructions for using Gospel Comparisons in daily study and in weekly group study appear as necessary in the study manual, in Gospel Comparisons, and in the leader guide.

JESUS IN THE GOSPELS takes participants deeper into Scripture as they look up and compare passages and make notes on them. Examining different accounts of the same or similar material brings richness and texture to study. Occasional words, phrases, or sentences printed in different colors will aid quick visual comparison of similarities and differences in Gospel accounts.

Video Component. The video is integral to each lesson and each weekly group session. The video segment for each lesson has two parts and begins and ends the weekly group session. The first part is a seven-to-ten-minute presentation by a Bible scholar or theologian on some topic or aspect of the subject treated in the lesson. It begins the session and is followed by discussion in small groups. Presentations by scholars enrich learning by taking viewers beyond their own reading and study.

The second part of the video segment absorbs the point of the lesson and celebrates it. It brings forward through art, music, words, and movement the Jesus in the week's Scripture. This one-to-three-minute portion of the video segment provides the closing to the weekly session; no discussion follows. Each two-part segment contributes to clarifying the distinctive angle of vision from which each Gospel presents Jesus. This thirty-segment set is available in either VHS or DVD. The price is the same for either set.

Leader Guide. Provides guidance for weekly group sessions that enables discussion in small groups of what persons have discovered in their individual reading and study. The leader guide understands the role of leader as guide of the process, giving special attention to time so all parts of the session plan are covered in each weekly session.

Two pages of guidance per session include directions for using the related two-part video segment, procedures for group activity and study related to daily assignments, guidance for use of Gospel Comparisons in group study of Scripture, and questions for discussion.

Other pages carry content aimed at helping the leader

create and maintain an environment of study and discussion that draws on the daily preparation of all group participants.

Procedures in the session plan keep the focus on the week's Scripture and describe activities suited to biblical material.

A consistent pattern and sequence of activity in the session plan from session to session allow the leader to concentrate on process and timing for specific activities. When the material is used as designed in the procedures described, neither process nor tangential issues take over.

The leader and group participants do the same daily reading of Scripture and taking of notes in preparation for the weekly group session.

No additional information is provided in the leader guide for presentation by the leader. The leader's role as process guide rather than information giver frees the leader to participate fully in small-group study and discussion. The leader's participating in all small-group study and discussion sends the message that the success of the group rests on all members.

The step in the weekly meeting when the group studies Scripture as a community recognizes the importance of and opens the way to reading Scripture aloud and hearing Scripture read aloud in the group. Instructions for group study of selected Scripture passages during the weekly meeting appear in the leader guide not in the study manual.

Certificate of Completion. A certificate to be presented at the end of the study to participants who have prepared for and participated in the thirty-week study

❖ recognizes commitment of time and discipline in study that backs up the expressed desire to better understand the Bible and
❖ confirms in recipients their sense of achievement and growth and their sense of experienced community.

When the certificate is presented in the presence of a congregation it serves as encouragement to others to undertake the study.

Emblem of Discipleship. A small cross to be given during the group's closing worship at the end of the study and to be carried in pocket or purse as a reminder of a call to discipleship from the Jesus in the Gospels. The cross, by its nature, bears the gospel message and reminds the holder through touch and sight that discipleship is costly. The cross serves as both symbol of commitment of time and study to learn of Jesus and as reminder of Jesus' challenge to take up the cross daily.

Think of Preparation in Terms of Commitment Not Convenience. JESUS IN THE GOSPELS takes critical scholarship seriously and therefore requires of participants skill in comparing and analyzing various Gospel passages, and biblical knowledge that enables participants to place particular New Testament passages about Jesus in their Old Testament context. In other words, participant preparation is rigorous.

DISCIPLE graduates will recognize that an increased amount of time is required for daily study because of the detailed reading called for in daily assignments. Completing daily assignments will involve use of the Bible, the study manual, and the Gospel Comparisons.

❖ Reading of assigned Scripture guided by suggestions of things to look for,
❖ writing notes on observations and insights,

❖ comparing Gospel accounts, and

❖ stating personal conclusions about the Jesus who has emerged from the participant's close reading of the Gospels make up the work of daily study.

In terms of time, participants should expect to spend forty-five to sixty minutes in daily study six days a week for thirty weeks and two and one-half hours per week attending and participating in the scheduled weekly meetings.

Group size of twelve persons plus a leader, and no fewer than eight and no more than fourteen, takes into account the importance of participant accountability for creating an atmosphere that fosters lively discussion and a sense of mutual support.

Bring Appropriate Expectations to This Study. What may participants expect of this study? Participants may expect to gain a fuller understanding of and appreciation for the four Gospels as richly textured portraits of Jesus.

Participants may expect to see the varying portraits of Jesus as opportunities to understand and appropriate more than one way of following Jesus.

Participants may expect to gain appreciation for Jesus; for the complexity of Jesus' historical time and place; and, in particular, for his Jewishness.

Participants may expect to be confronted weekly by Jesus and summoned to deeper allegiance and loyalty to Jesus.

Participants may expect that this study of Jesus, while taking critical scholarship seriously, will enrich rather than impoverish their understanding of Jesus.

Participants may expect to understand what is at stake in doctrinal claims about Jesus that have roots in Scripture.

Participants may expect to converse more seriously than in the past about their Christian heritage in Jesus, to be able to take a stand—this is what we believe.

Participants may expect to continually confront the question, What constitutes my followship?

In terms of approach to study, participants may expect daily disciplined reading and study of Scripture with growing attention to detail.

Participants may expect regularly to use their Bible, their study manual, and their Gospel Comparisons together in daily study.

Participants may expect to learn anew that the Old Testament permeates the whole Bible, that the Gospel writers and Jesus relied on the Old Testament; it was their Scripture, the only Scripture they knew.

Participants may expect a growing appreciation of the Gospels as literature in their own right—Luke really knows how to tell a good story!

Participants may expect to be surprised, to be shocked, to be made uncomfortable, to be stretched, to be awed, to be comforted, and to experience hope and peace.

Training Precedes Ordering. The first leader of JESUS IN THE GOSPELS in any DISCIPLE-enrolled church must attend JESUS IN THE GOSPELS training. A DISCIPLE-enrolled church may order JESUS IN THE GOSPELS materials *after* at least one person from the church has attended a JESUS IN THE GOSPELS training seminar.

The initial cost to a church is the cost of training only. The training fee for one person includes training, accommodations, meals, and materials used in the training—

handbook,
study manual,
Gospel Comparisons, and
leader guide.

The training fee is the same for each person trained from a church. The training fee does not include cost of travel to and from the training site. Persons attending a training seminar must attend the entire seminar in order to be prepared to teach and to receive the available Continuing Education Unit.

If a pastor or a layperson has attended a JESUS IN THE GOSPELS training seminar or has completed the thirty-week study and moves to a new church or charge, that person's moving to the new church or charge makes the church or charge eligible for ordering the JESUS IN THE GOSPELS kit. Persons who complete the thirty-week study of JESUS IN THE GOSPELS may lead subsequent groups. However we highly recommend that they attend a JESUS IN THE GOSPELS training seminar.

After at least one person from a local church is trained, the church may order the JESUS IN THE GOSPELS kit which includes the materials necessary for one study group—

thirteen handbooks,

thirteen study manuals,

thirteen Gospel Comparisons,

one leader guide,

one set of the VHS or DVD video component,

thirteen certificates,

thirteen crosses—

and may order as many additional handbooks; study manuals; Gospel Comparisons; leader guides; certificates; crosses; and, depending on the number of study groups and group schedules, additional video components. The kit must be the first purchase by any church.

JESUS IN THE GOSPELS materials will not be shipped automatically. Forms for ordering the JESUS IN THE GOSPELS kit will be available at the training seminars. Clergy or laypersons attending the training should come with authority to order the materials at the seminar. Or persons may send the order form by fax after returning home from training.

Materials will be shipped approximately one week after an order has been received.

JESUS IN THE GOSPELS materials are sold only to DISCIPLE-enrolled churches, not to individuals or groups, and only through the training and ordering process described here, not in Cokesbury stores.

Churches can recover some of the cost of the study by inviting group members to pay for their own study manuals and Gospel Comparisons. Each participant needs a study manual and a Gospel Comparisons. Participants will write in them weekly and will keep them at the end of the study.

Contact us by telephone at 800-251-8591, by fax at 615-749-6049, or through our web page at www.cokesbury.com/services/disciple.asp, or return the response card from this handbook for information on training fees, training dates and locations, and for prices of JESUS IN THE GOSPELS materials.

Why is training called for if the leader has already attended a DISCIPLE training seminar? Close reading of Scripture guided by suggestions of things to look for and regular comparing of Gospel texts using the Bible, the Gospel Comparisons, and the study manual commentary will be new experiences for DISCIPLE graduates participating in JESUS IN THE GOSPELS. The fact that the format of the study manual is different from the familiar DISCIPLE format and layout and requires a different approach to daily study— plus the addition of the new Gospel Comparisons—means that participants will look to the leader for guidance in using the materials. A training seminar will prepare leaders to assist participants in their groups in knowing how to use the suggestions of things to look for when reading Scripture and for using Gospel Comparisons for spotting differences and similarities in Gospel accounts of the same story.

- ❖ Training creates the small-group situation for practice in studying and using the materials and practice in planning to lead weekly group study.
- ❖ Actual use of the materials in small groups teaches the function of each component and the relationship among the components. Use of the materials teaches how the parts of each component fit into the procedure and schedule of a weekly group meeting.
- ❖ Practice with the materials in the small group demonstrates use of time, and adherence to schedule and format demonstrates that the program is self-contained: JESUS IN THE GOSPELS materials provide everything needed for productive and challenging study of the Gospels.
- ❖ Training demonstrates that small-group discussion and study works when persons have completed their study and preparation, that disciplined study and preparation and commitment to schedule, procedure, and format bring intended results.
- ❖ Participants experience the bonding that takes place in the small group even in the short training time and can anticipate such bonding in their own groups.
- ❖ Training emphasizes that the leader and the group members make the same preparation and participate equally in the weekly discussion and study.

Prior to training, persons registered to attend training receive assignment booklets for use in preparation for training. Laity and clergy leave training knowing they are equipped to lead JESUS IN THE GOSPELS.

Bible
the Foundation

Study of God's word lays the foundation for the work of ministry by God's people. DISCIPLE offers congregations a challenge and a promise. The challenge is to see the regular, in-depth study of Scripture as the foundation for making disciples and doing ministry. The promise is that all who submit themselves to examination by Scripture will, with the aid of the Holy Spirit, be changed. For congregations desiring their way of life to be transformed by the way of Christ, commitment to study of the Bible is the first and foundational step.

Christian Doctrines the Building Blocks

Study of Christian doctrine provides the building blocks of Christian teachings for determining the work of ministry. CHRISTIAN BELIEVER offers congregations a study of classical doctrines that results in voice, ear, eye, and heart attuned to the language of the Christian faith. Concepts and images in Scripture, words and ideas in creeds and hymns, symbols and song in worship—these elements constitute the legacy out of which a congregation's ministries take shape and find purpose.

CHRISTIAN BELIEVER

Jesus Christ the Cornerstone

Study of JESUS IN THE GOSPELS keeps the work of ministry aligned with Jesus' mission and message. This first study in the DISCIPLE Second Generation Studies line carries forward the philosophy and the ideals that shaped DISCIPLE—high commitment, long-term, disciplined study. As a cornerstone provides stability for a structure, so this study fixes participants firmly in the witness of the four Gospels and holds them accountable to the Jesus who emerges from that witness.

Foundation, building blocks, cornerstone—the basics for building solid Christians.

JESUS IN THE GOSPELS